Careers without College

Dental Hygienist

by Charnan Simon

Content Consultant:
Lois Ulrey
Manager, Dental Hygiene Education
American Dental Hygienists' Association

CAPSTONE
HIGH/LOW BOOKS
an imprint of Capstone Press

CAPSTONE PRESS

818 North Willow Street • Mankato, Minnesota 56001
http://www.capstone-press.com

Copyright © 1998 Capstone Press. All rights reserved.
No part of this book may be reproduced without written permission from the publisher.
The publisher takes no responsibility for the use of any of the materials or methods described in this book, nor for the products thereof.
Printed in the United States of America.

Library of Congress Cataloging-in-Publication Data
Simon, Charnan.
    Dental hygienist/by Charnan Simon.
       p. cm.--(Careers without college)
    Includes bibliographical references and index.
    Summary: Outlines the educational requirements, duties, salary, employment outlook, and possible future positions of dental hygienists.
    ISBN 1-56065-701-4
    1. Dental hygiene--Vocational guidance--Juvenile literature.
[1. Dental hygiene--Vocational guidance. 2. Vocational guidance.]
I. Title. II. Series: Careers without college (Mankato, Minn.)
RK60.S55 1998
617.6'01'023--DC21

97-35230
CIP
AC r97

Photo credits:
Peter S. Ford, 32
I.B.A. Photography/Peggy Walsh, 12
International Stock/Randy Masser, 22
Maguire PhotograFX/Joseph P. Maguire, 35
Leslie O'Shaughnessy, 11, 14, 17, 19, 24, 27, 28, 30, 36, 41, 44
Photo Network/Esbin-Anderson, 6, 39; Tom McCarthy, 9; Mark Sherman, 4;
  Phillip Roullard, 43
Unicorn Stock Photos/Chuck Schmeiser, cover
Valan Photos/Wouterloot-Gregoire, 21

Table of Contents

Fast Facts 5

Chapter 1   What Dental Hygienists Do ... 7

Chapter 2   What the Job Is Like 15

Chapter 3   Training 21

Chapter 4   Salary and Job Outlook 29

Chapter 5   Where the Job Can Lead 37

Words to Know 42

To Learn More 45

Useful Addresses 46

Internet Sites 47

Index 48

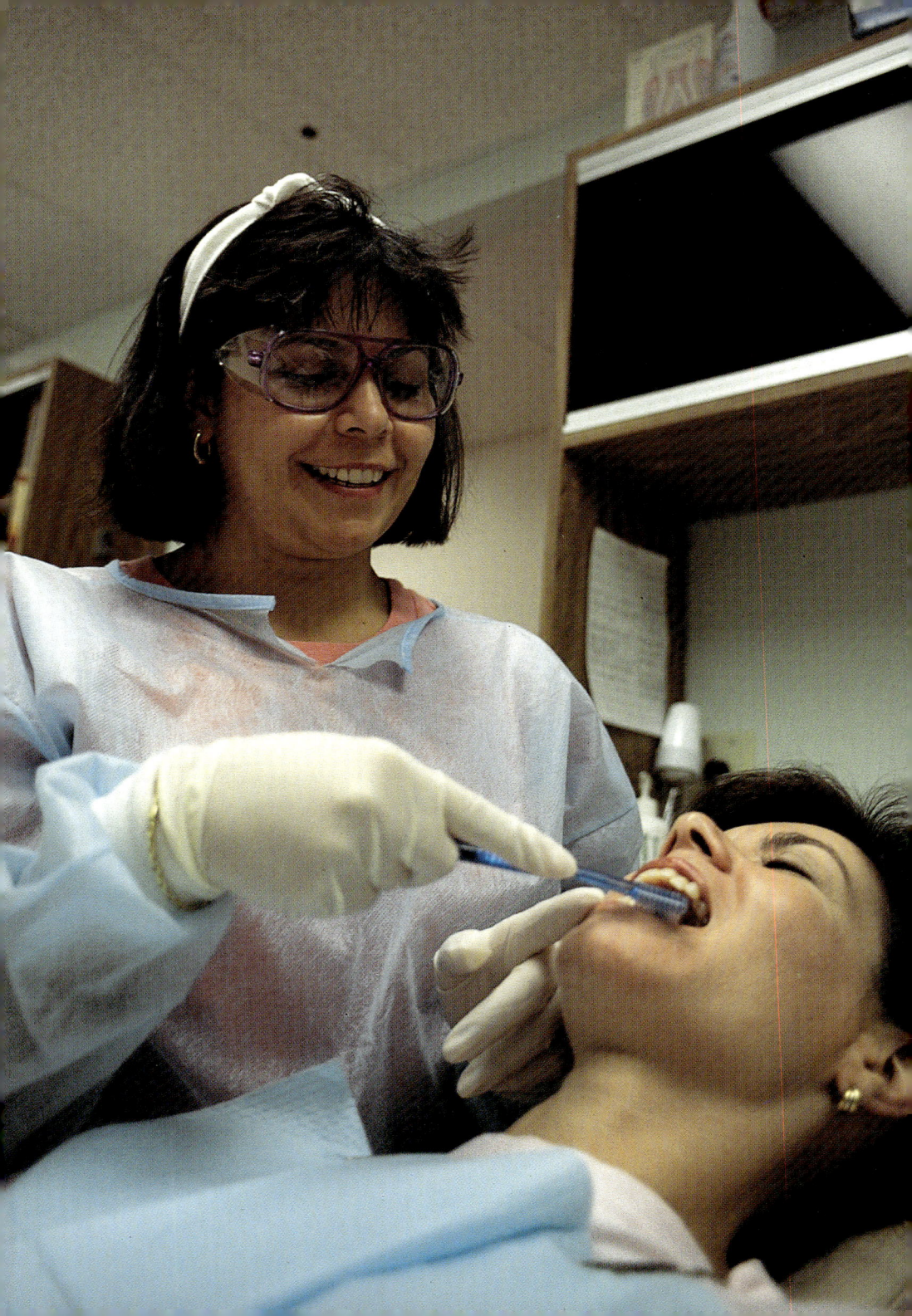

Fast Facts

Career Title —————————————— Dental Hygienist

Minimum Educational Requirement —————————— Two-year associate's degree

Licensure Requirement ——————— State licensing examination

U.S. Salary Range ————————— $15,200 to $31,500

Canadian Salary Range ——————— $15,200 to $56,900
(Canadian dollars)

U.S. Job Outlook —————————— Much faster than the average

Canadian Job Outlook ——————— Much faster than the average

DOT Cluster ——————————————— Professional, technical, and
(Dictionary of Occupational Titles)   managerial occupations

DOT Number ——————————————— 078.361-010

GOE Number ——————————————— 10.02.02
(Guide for Occupational Exploration)

NOC ———————————————————— 3222
(National Occupational Classification—Canada)

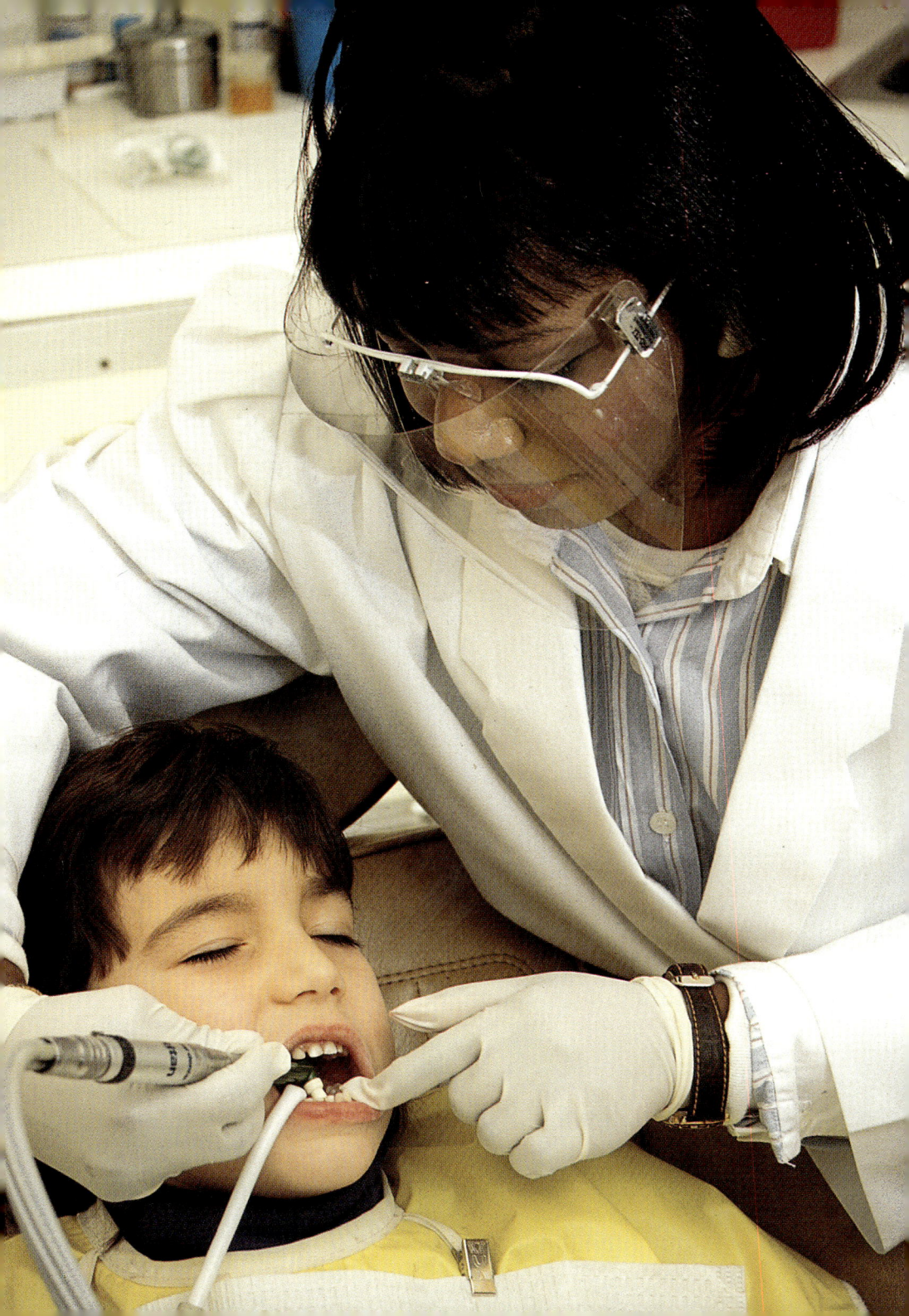

Chapter 1

What Dental Hygienists Do

Dental hygienists help dentists in many ways. Their main duty is to clean patients' teeth. Hygienists also teach patients how to care for their teeth. Keeping teeth clean and taking care of them prevents tooth decay and gum disease. Tooth decay is a process that turns healthy teeth rotten. Gum disease is an illness in the areas of firm pink flesh around the teeth.

Dental hygienists clean people's teeth.

On the Job

Hygienists clean people's teeth. Hygienists remove plaque and calculus from teeth. Plaque is a soft coating that forms on teeth that can cause tooth decay. Calculus is hardened plaque. Hygienists also remove stains. Stains are colored spots on teeth.

Dental hygienists also polish and floss teeth. Floss means to pull a thin strand of thread between teeth to clean them.

Dental hygienists keep careful records on each patient. They write down all possible signs of decay or disease. They record the locations of all cavities and fillings. A cavity is a hole in a tooth caused by decay. A filling is matter put into a cavity to stop decay. Hygienists must be exact in keeping these charts. Dentists depend on these charts to decide how to treat patients' teeth.

Dental hygienists teach their patients about tooth care.

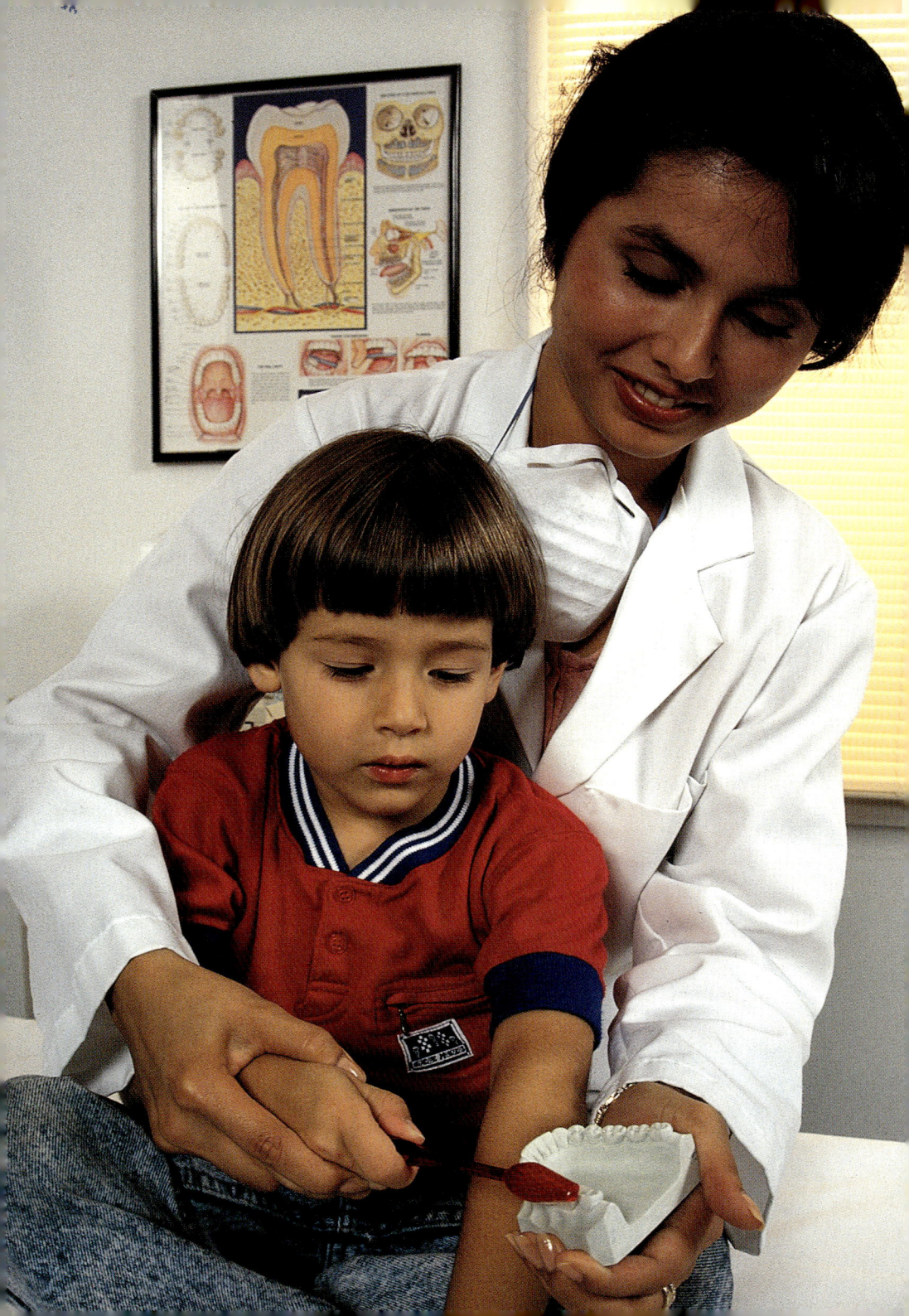

Preventive Dentistry

Dental hygienists practice preventive dentistry. Preventive dentistry means keeping teeth healthy to prevent diseases.

Dental hygienists teach patients how to care for their teeth. They show patients how to brush and floss their teeth properly. Brushing and flossing keep teeth clean. This prevents tooth decay and gum disease.

Hygienists also offer advice on which foods to eat and which foods not to eat. They ask patients to visit dentists regularly.

Hygienists apply sealants to seal teeth against decay. Sealants are coatings that cover the chewing surfaces of teeth. They keep disease away from the teeth. Dental hygienists also apply fluoride treatments. Fluoride is a chemical that helps prevent tooth decay.

Dental hygienists show patients how to brush and floss their teeth.

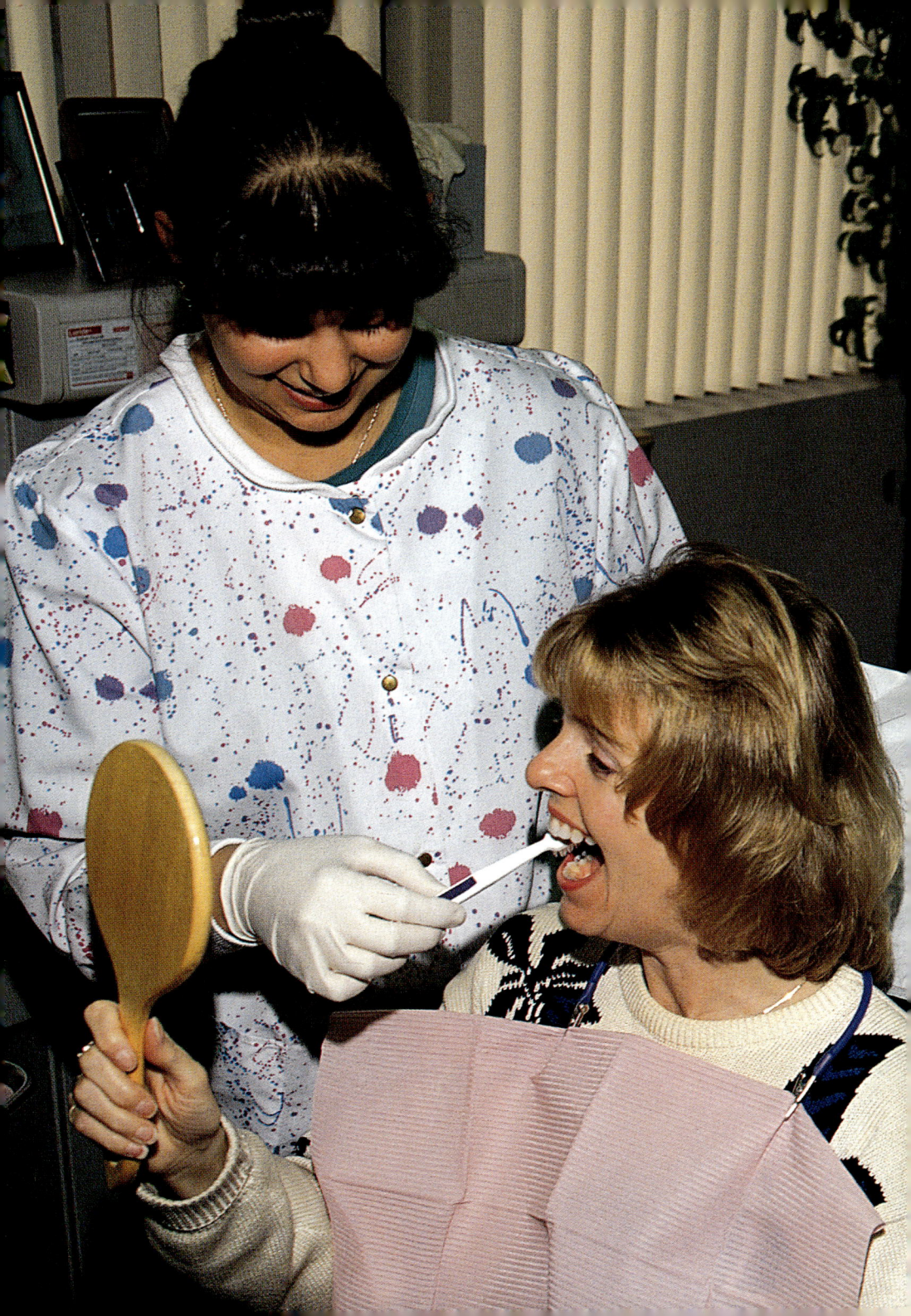

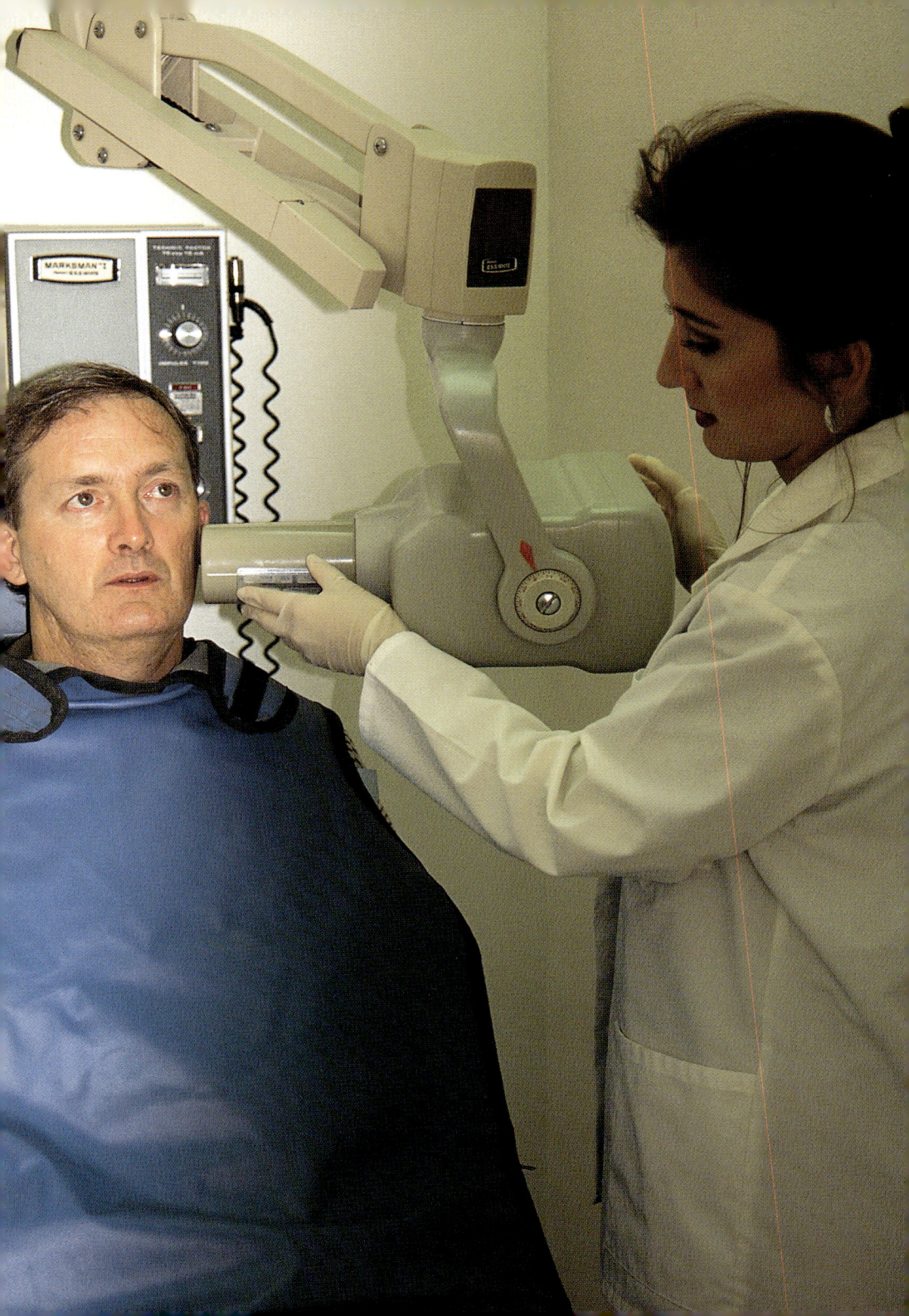

Other Duties

Dental hygienists may have other duties as well. They take X rays of patients' teeth. An X ray is a photograph of the inside of a person's body. Dentists study these X rays for signs of tooth decay or disease.

Hygienists also help dentists find cavities. Hygienists sometimes prepare the matter used to fill a cavity. Some dental hygienists give pain-killing shots. Patients need these shots when dentists pull teeth or fill cavities.

Sometimes dental hygienists perform general office work. They may answer telephones or set up appointments. They may fill out insurance forms and send out bills. Usually a receptionist or office manager performs these duties.

Dental hygienists take X rays of patients' teeth.

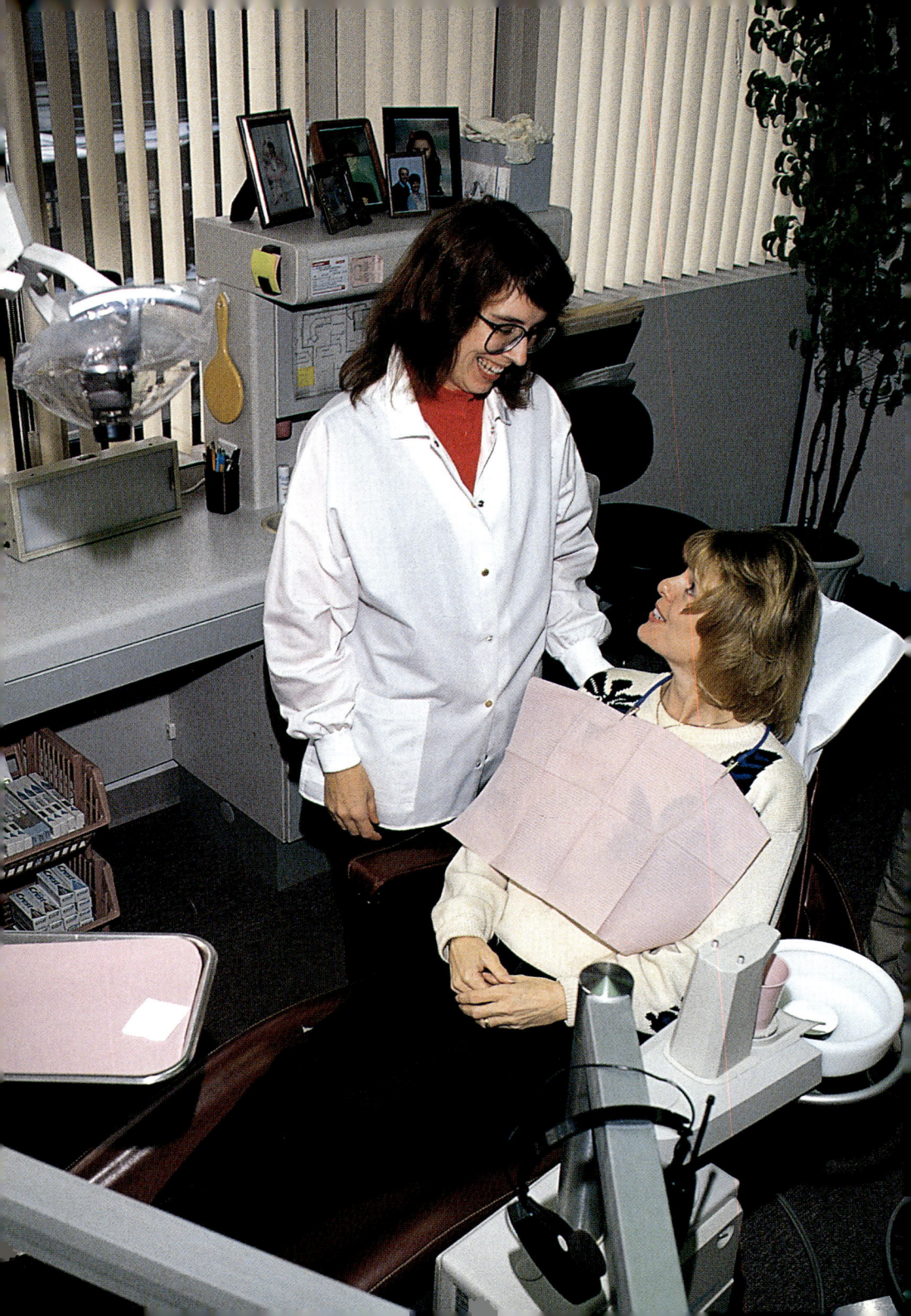

Chapter 2

What the Job Is Like

Dental hygienists work with people every day. They explain to patients what will happen during their visits. Dental hygienists talk to patients to help them relax. Dental hygienists are gentle when cleaning patients' teeth.

Dental hygienists must pay attention to details. They need to choose the correct dental tools and use them correctly.

Dental hygienists help patients relax.

Dental hygienists wear masks, gloves, and safety glasses. These articles help protect hygienists and patients from infection. Infection is an illness caused by germs. Hygienists also protect themselves when they work with X rays or give pain-killing shots.

Work Settings

Dental hygienists may choose to work full-time or part-time. Full-time means working 40 hours per week. Many dentists need hygienists to work only two or three days each week. Hygienists who want to work full-time often work for more than one dentist. Other hygienists prefer to work fewer hours. Some dental hygienists work evening and weekend hours.

Most dental hygienists work in private dental offices. Dentists oversee the work of hygienists. Some hygienists work for the military. Others work in schools or hospitals.

Dental hygienists wear masks, gloves, and safety glasses.

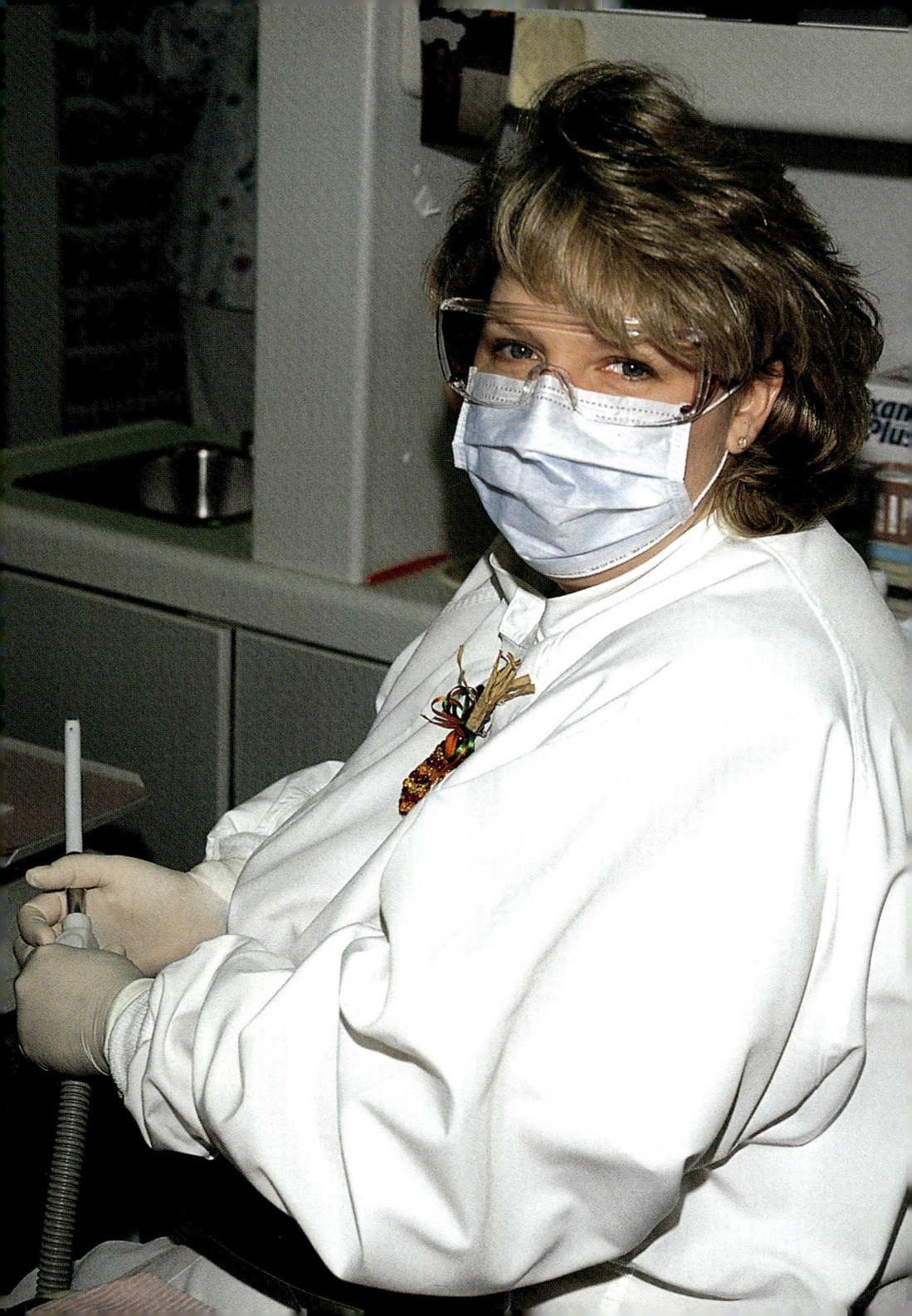

Other Work Opportunities

Public health dental hygienists work for local, state, or national governments. Sometimes they clean government workers' teeth. Sometimes they create dental health programs for the public. These programs teach people how to take care of their teeth and gums.

Some dental hygienists do research or teach in colleges. Research hygienists study how dental products work. They try to discover new dental treatments. Research hygienists also study the best ways to provide patient care. Dental hygienists who teach work at dental hygiene schools. They prepare students for careers as hygienists.

Research hygienists study the best ways to provide patient care.

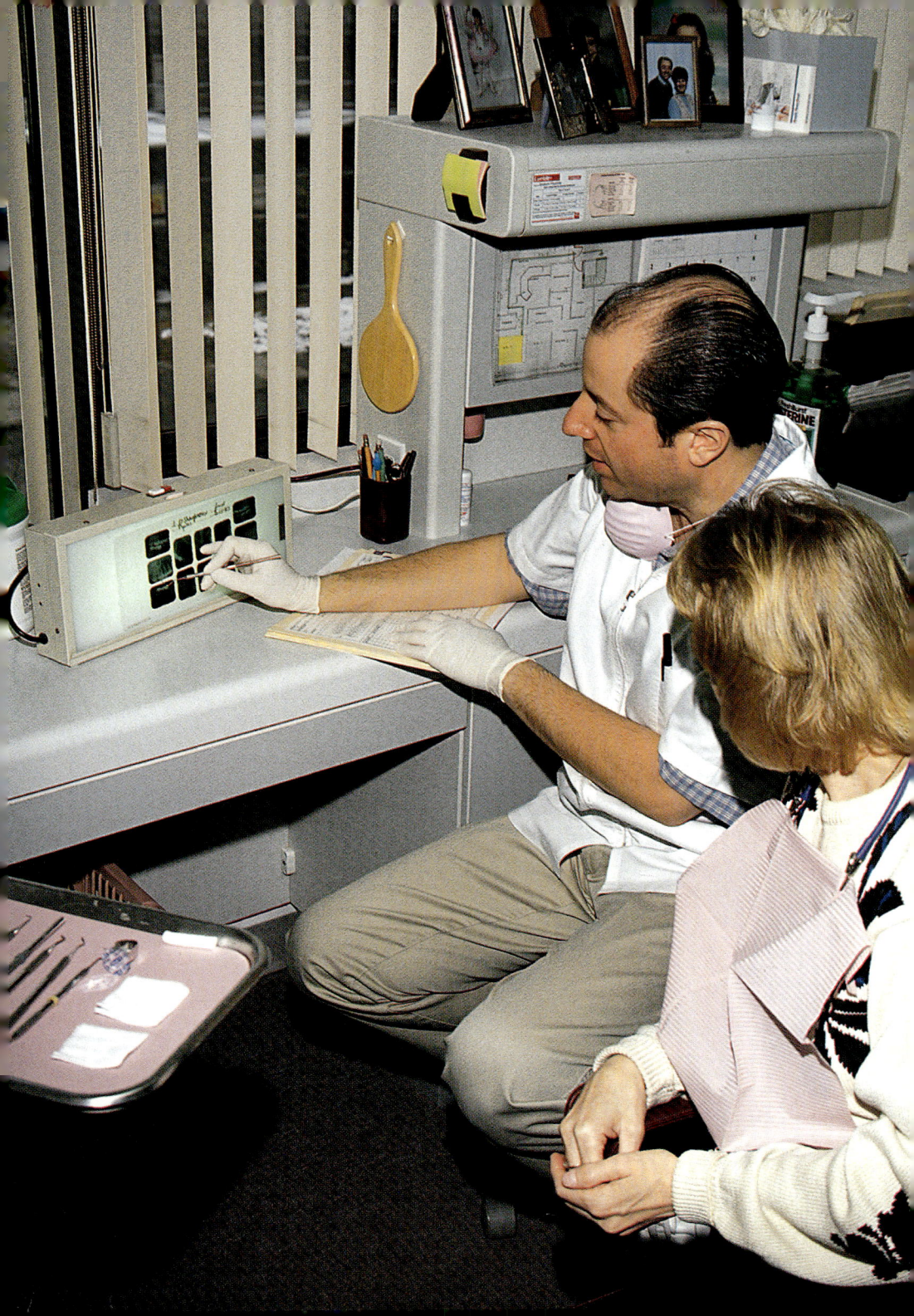

Chapter 3

Training

People who want to be dental hygienists should study hard in high school. They should take science and math courses. These classes will help them prepare for training as a dental hygienist. Dental hygienist training usually takes two years. Dental hygiene students must study hard to succeed.

Dental hygiene students must study hard to succeed.

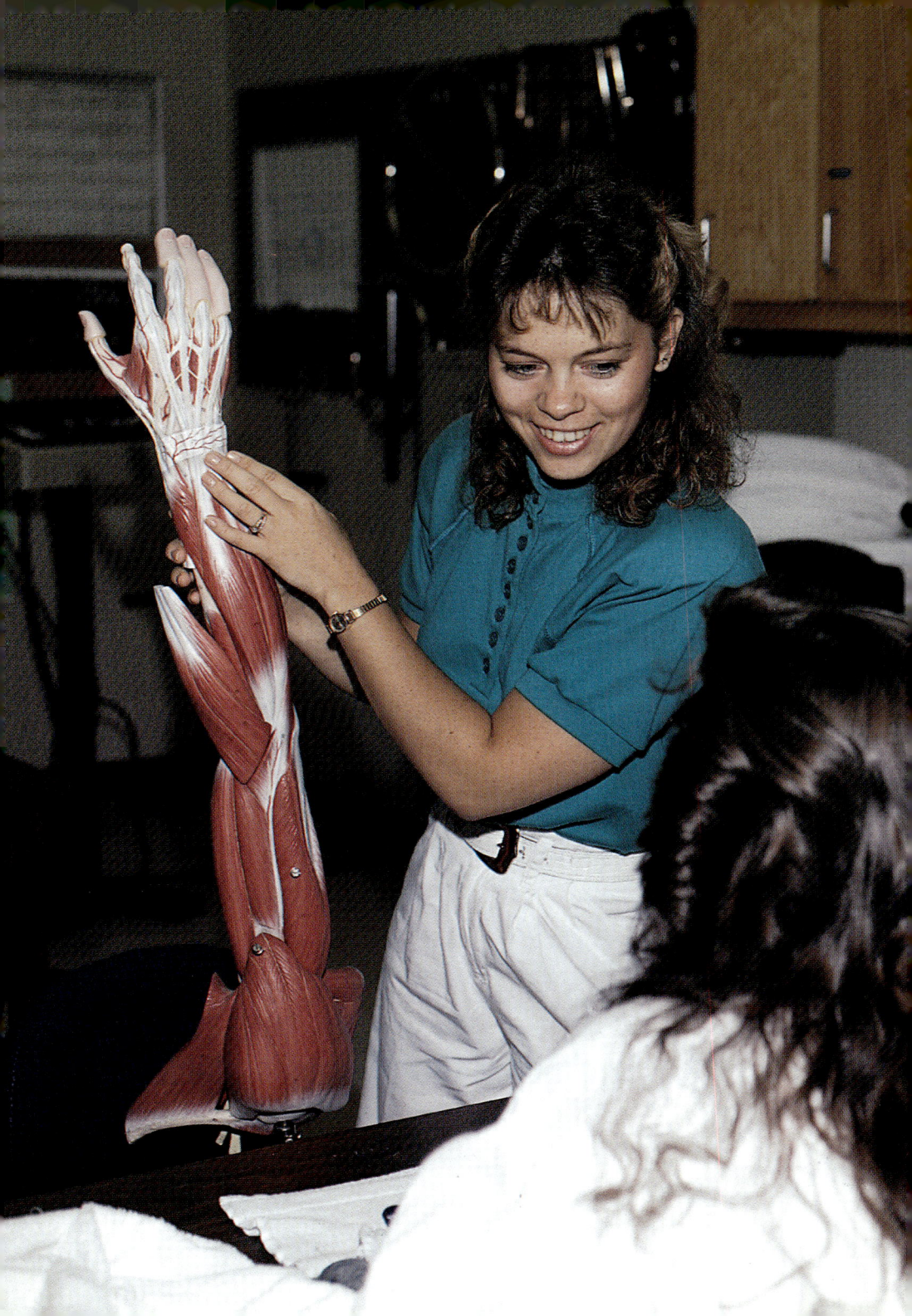

Dental Hygienist Programs

There are two ways to train as a dental hygienist. Students can attend two-year programs. Students who finish these programs earn associate's degrees or certificates in dental hygiene. A degree is a title given to a person for completing a course of study. Many approved schools offer two-year programs.

People can also finish four-year college programs. These students earn bachelor's degrees in dental hygiene. Many employers like to hire hygienists who have completed four-year programs.

Some dental hygiene schools ask each student to take a test before they enroll. The test shows if the students have the proper skills to be a dental hygienist. Students who do well on their tests are likely to become good dental hygienists.

Dental hygiene students take many science courses. They learn about anatomy. Anatomy is

Dental hygiene students learn about anatomy.

the study of the body. They learn about diseases that affect the teeth and gums.

Dental hygiene students also take practical courses. They learn how to use dental tools. They also practice working with patients who come to the dental hygiene school.

Becoming Licensed

Graduating from dental hygiene school is only the first step. All dental hygienists in the United States must pass a licensing exam. A license is a paper that gives permission to do something. State governments license hygienists. Hygienists take the test in the state in which they wish to practice. Hygienists can practice as registered dental hygienists (R.D.H.) after they pass the exam.

Licensing exams have two parts. First, students must pass a written test. This test is called the National Board Dental Hygiene Exam. The Joint Commission on National Dental Examinations gives the test. Next, students must pass a clinical test. Each state or region gives this test. It

All dental hygienists in the United States must pass a licensing exam.

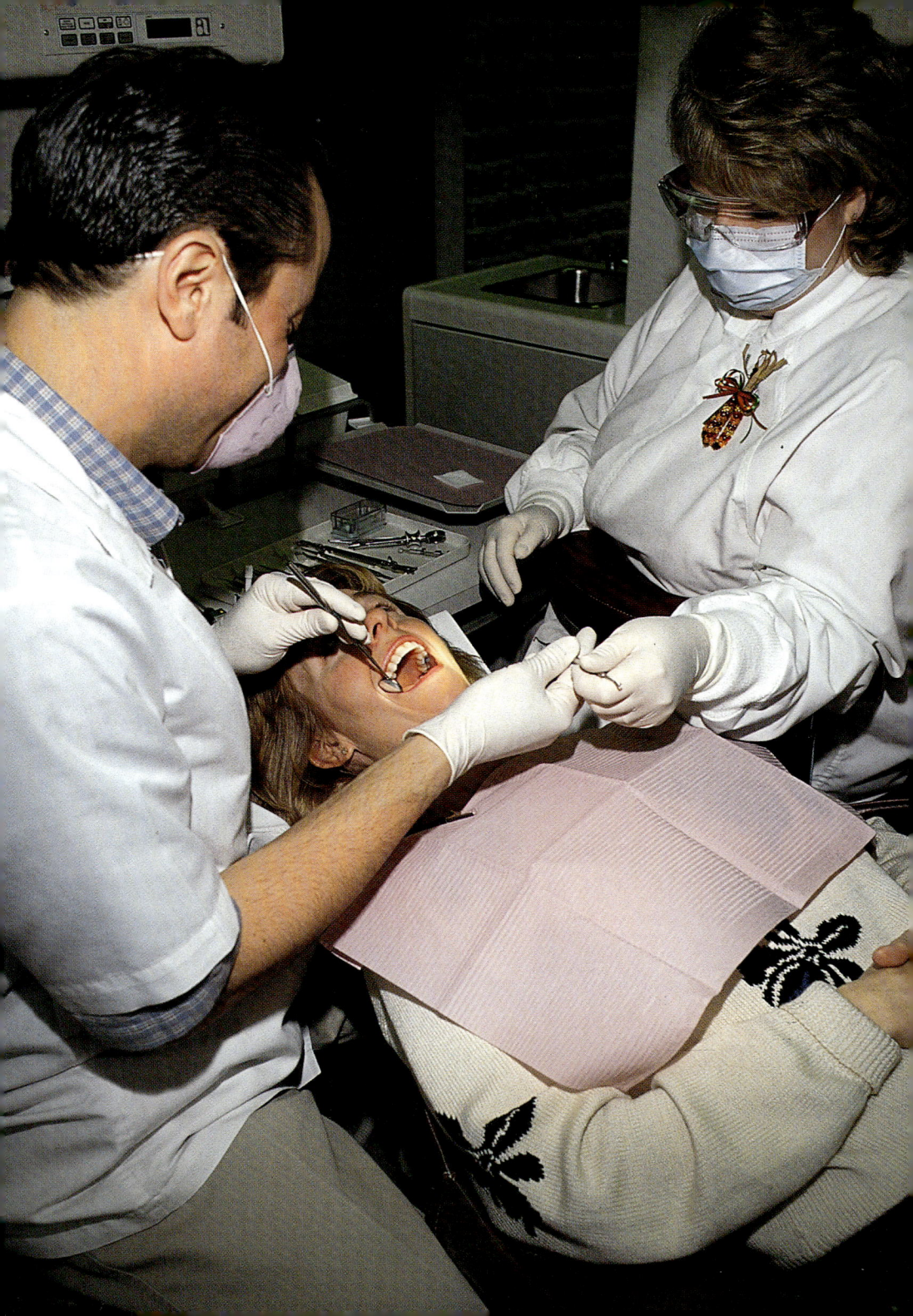

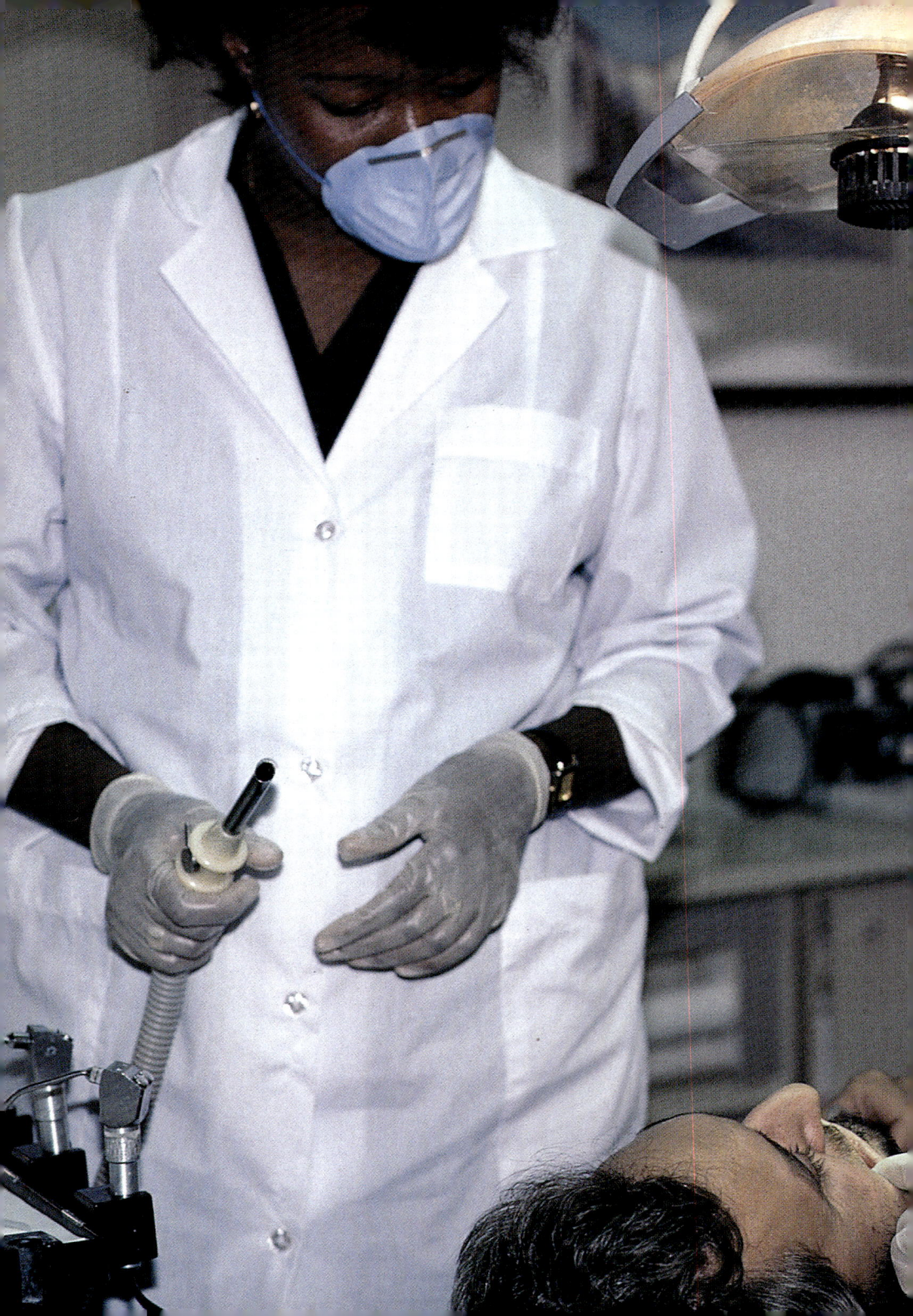

measures how well students perform as dental hygienists. Licensing requirements vary from province to province in Canada.

Licensed dental hygienists often take continuing education courses. These courses teach new dental procedures. They teach about developments in dental care. They offer information about government rules and regulations. Good dental hygienists keep learning throughout their careers.

What to Do Now

High school students who are interested in the field should look for part-time work as a dental assistant. Assistants help dentists and dental hygienists. They greet patients. They help them into examining rooms. Assistants hand instruments to dentists during treatment.

A dental assistant can learn a lot about dentistry. This experience might make it easier to get into dental hygiene school.

Dental assistants hand instruments to dentists during treatments.

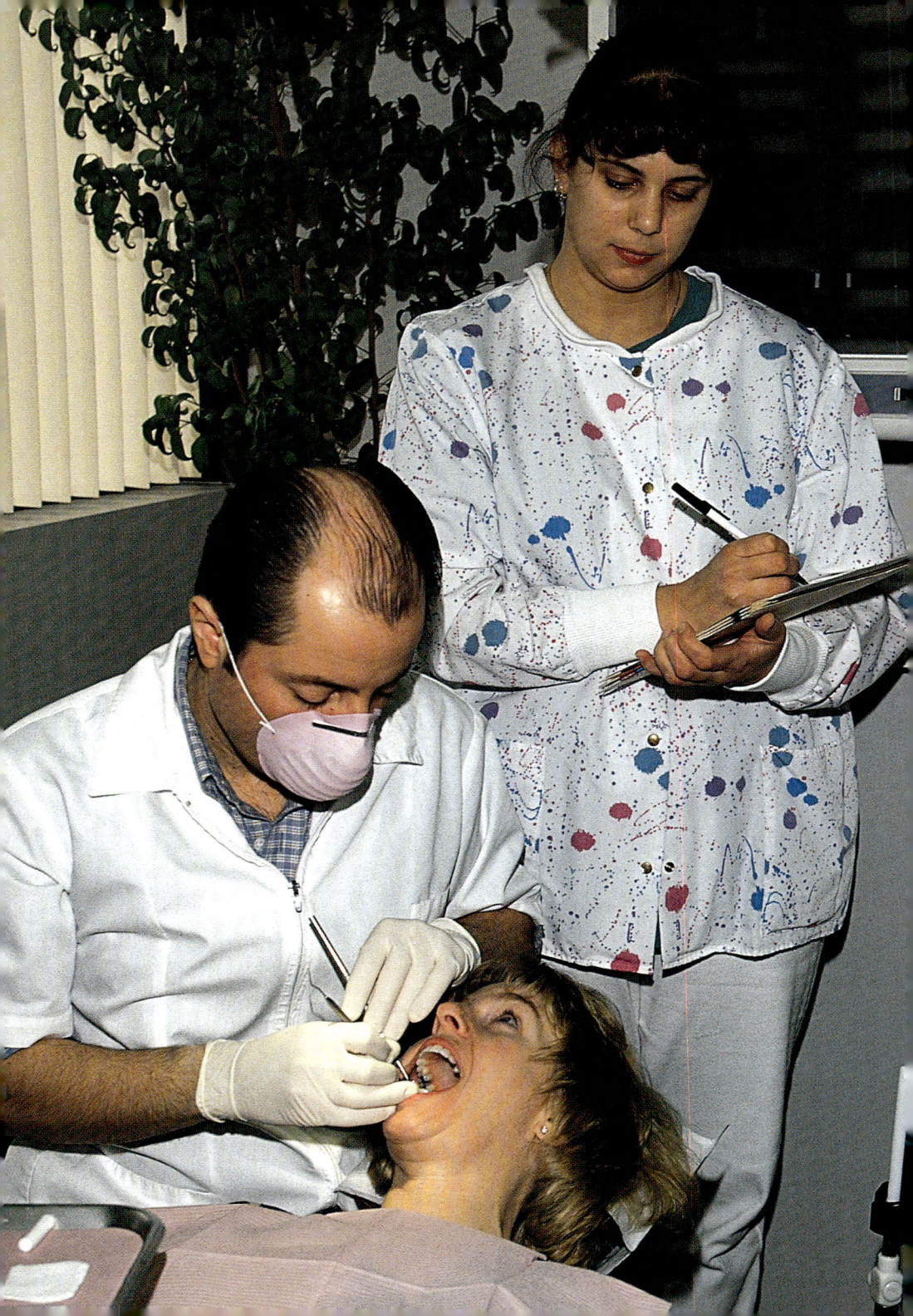

Chapter 4

Salary and Job Outlook

Dental hygienists' pay depends on their education, their experience, and where they work. Dental hygienists earn from $15,200 to $31,500 per year in the United States. In Canada, hygienists earn from $15,200 to $56,900 per year.

Dental hygienists who work as researchers or teachers sometimes earn more than other hygienists. Some dental hygienists return to

Dental hygienists' pay depends on their education and experience.

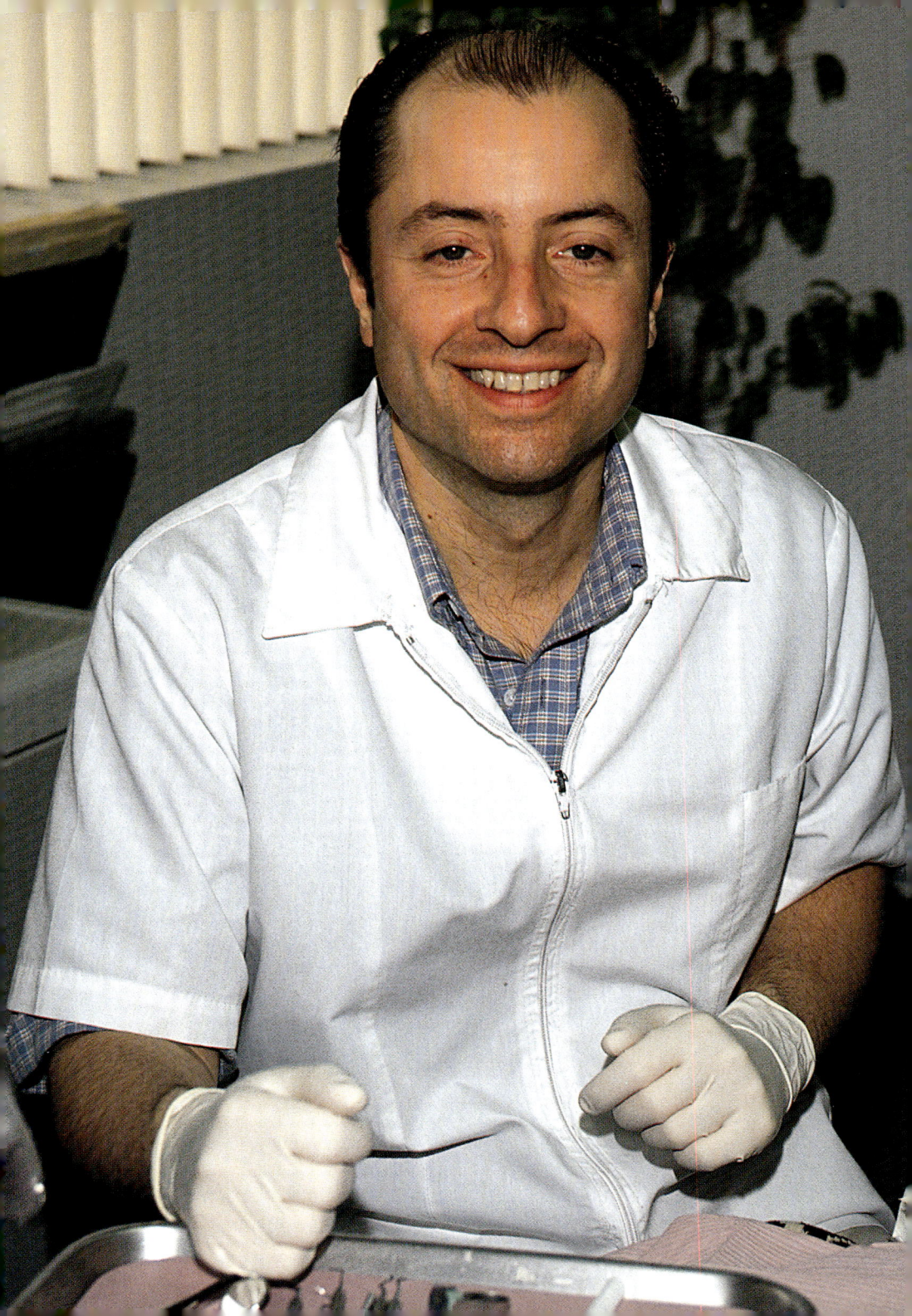

school for advanced degrees such as master's degrees or doctorate degrees. Hygienists with these degrees can be researchers or teachers in colleges.

Dental hygienists may be paid on an hourly, daily, or weekly basis. Hygienists who work on a weekly basis are salaried employees. Full-time hygienists earn about $20.40 per hour. Part-time hygienists earn about $24.50 per hour. Part-time hygienists make more per hour. But they usually do not get paid vacations or other benefits.

Benefits and Commissions

Full-time dental hygienists are usually the only hygienists who receive benefits. A benefit is a payment or service paid by an employer in addition to a salary or wage. Hygienists may receive health insurance, paid holidays, and paid sick days. Health insurance is protection

Dental hygienists may be paid on an hourly, daily, or weekly basis.

31

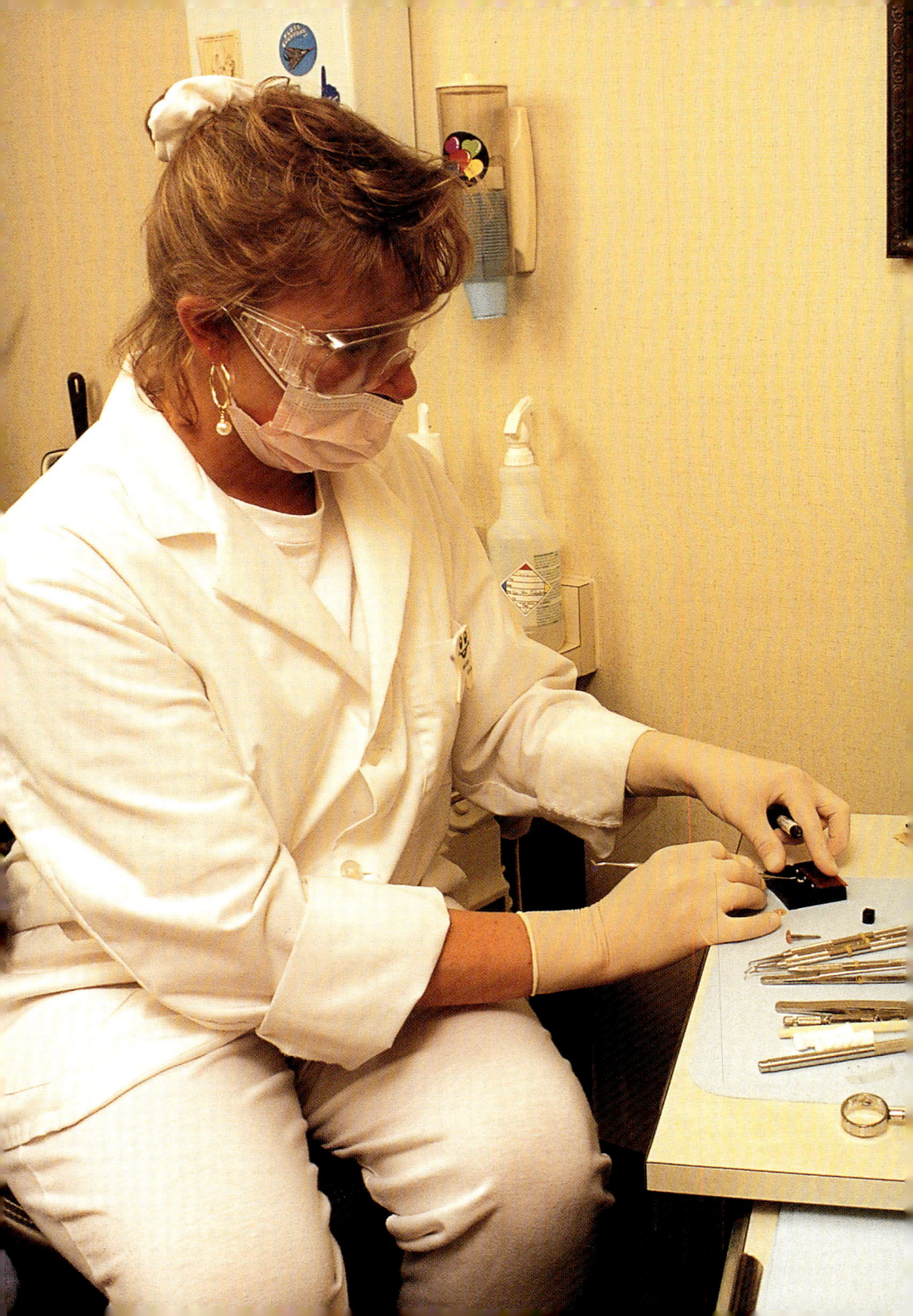

against the costs of getting sick. People pay a small amount each month to insurance companies. The insurance companies pay most of the bills if a person gets sick. Benefits vary from office to office.

Dental hygienists who work in schools or for public health agencies generally get excellent benefits. Sometimes they receive more vacation time or better insurance. However, they may not earn as much per hour as hygienists who work in dentists' offices.

Some dental hygienists work on commission. This means they receive amounts for each patient they work with. The more patients a hygienist sees, the higher salary he or she earns. Some hygienists receive a combination of salary and commission.

Dental hygienists who have worked for several years may earn more than beginning hygienists.

Job Outlook

The need for dental hygienists is growing fast. Dentists will probably hire more hygienists as their workloads increase.

The need for dental hygienists should continue to grow in the near future. More people are keeping their teeth healthy as they age. These people need regular, professional dental care from skilled dental hygienists.

Dental hygienists who work in schools may receive excellent benefits.

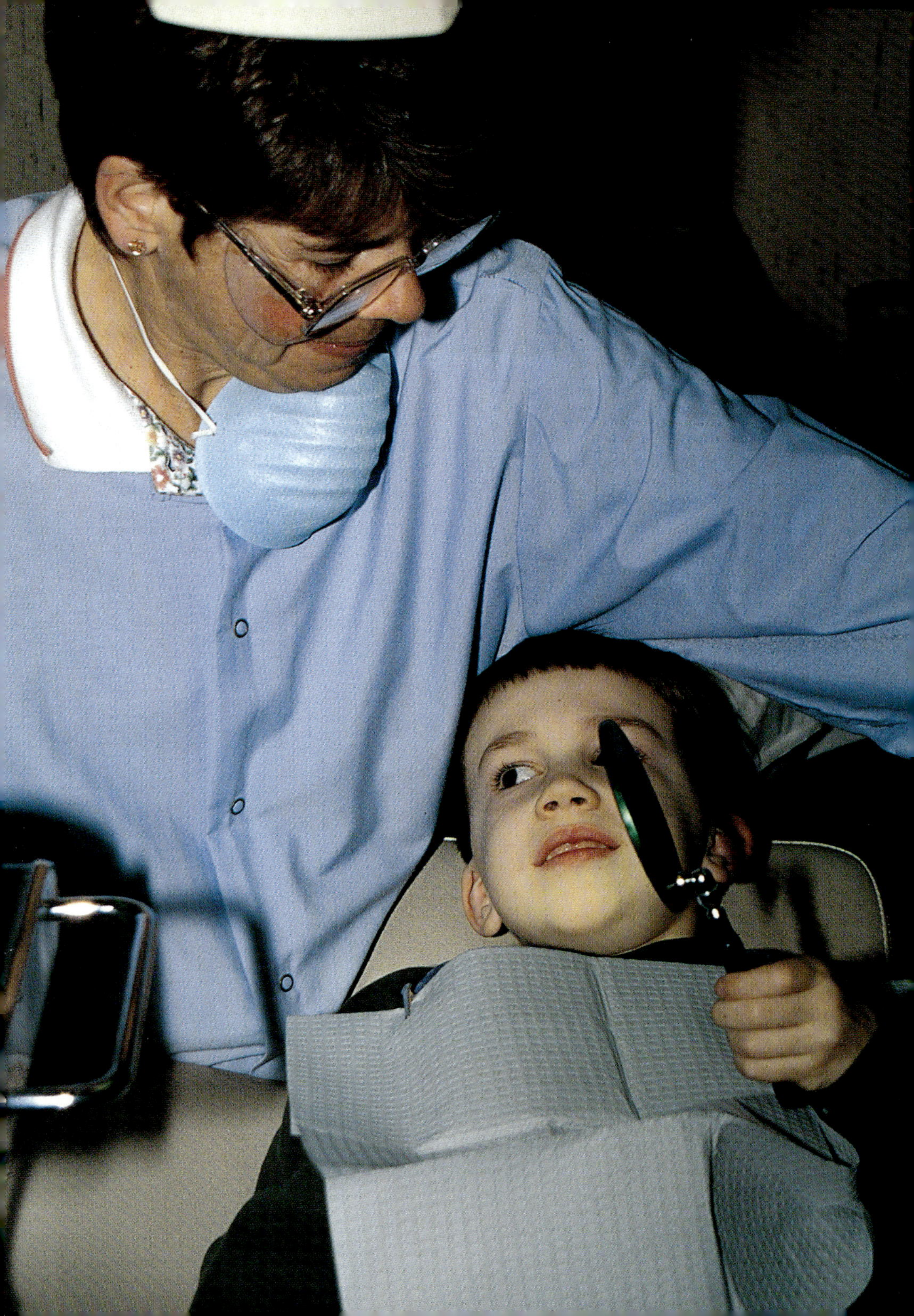

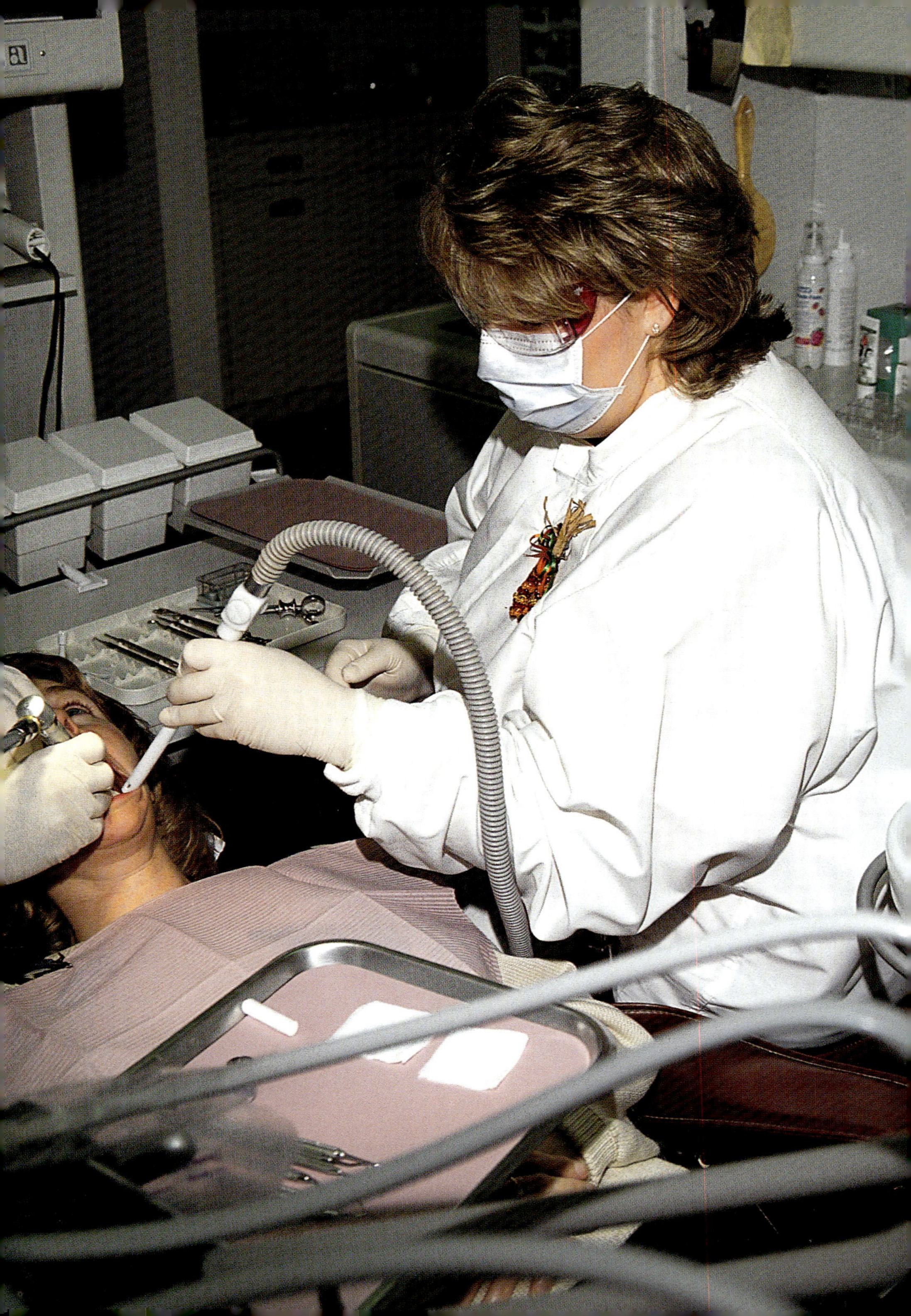

Chapter 5

Where the Job Can Lead

Dental hygienists can advance in many ways. Experienced hygienists may get more responsibilities. Hygienists can also receive more training. Hygienists may become teachers. Dental hygiene is a growing field. It offers many opportunities.

Dental hygienists can advance in many ways.

Promotions Within the Office

Full-time dental hygienists can receive salary raises. Dental hygienists can earn more money with more experience. They can also become supervisors of dental assistants in large dental practices.

Some dental hygienists become managers. They might run dental offices. Others might become heads of government dental programs. These people must have good organizational skills. They must be able to manage people and money.

Additional Training

Hygienists can advance in the field by getting more education. Some dental hygiene schools offer master's degree programs. Hygienists with master's degrees can become teachers.

Dental hygienists also might earn more money by moving to different offices. Dental

Dental hygienists may earn more money with more experience.

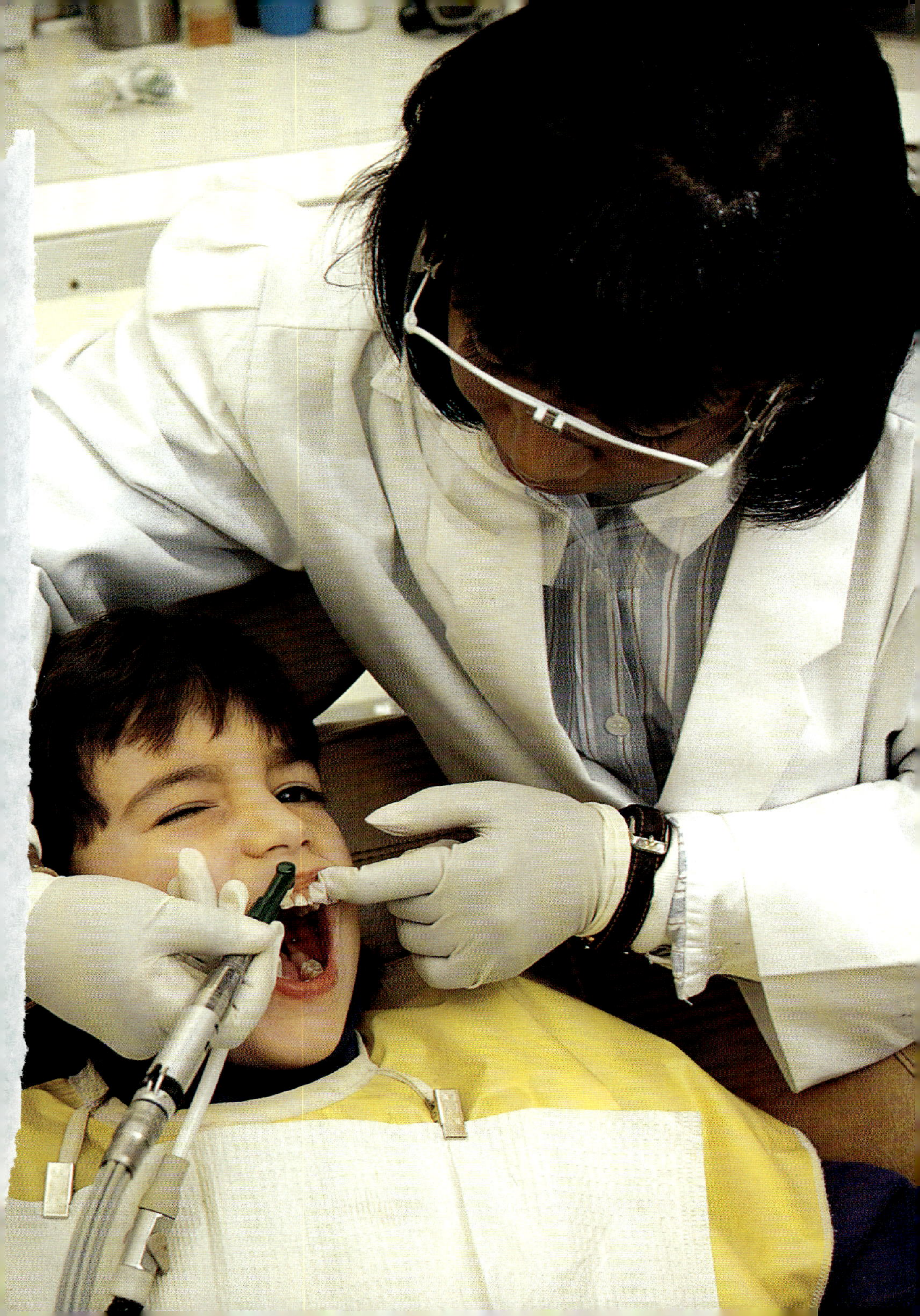

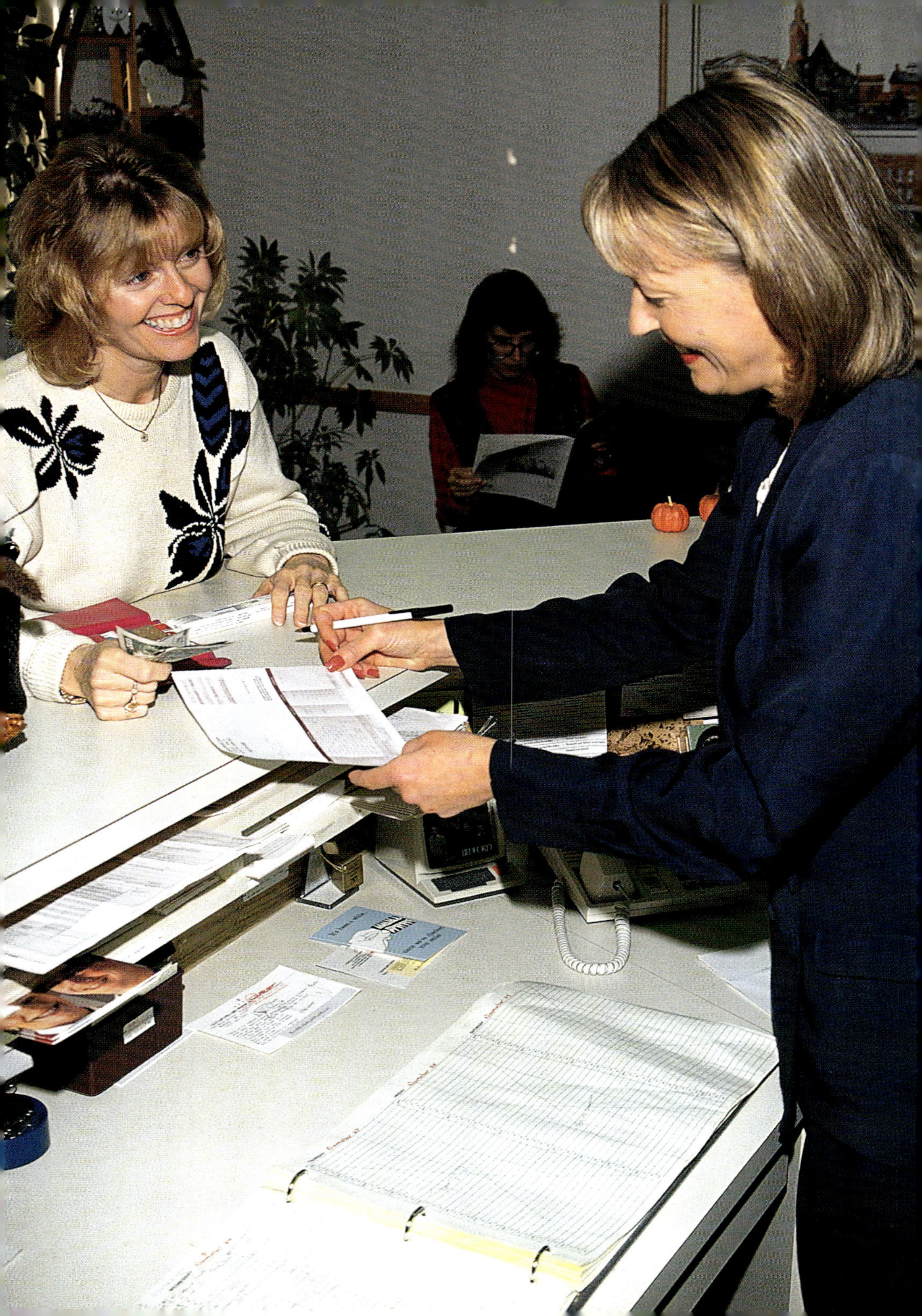

hygienists can work in all types of dentist's offices. Some offices specialize in certain types of dentistry. Specialize means to focus on one area of work. These offices might specialize in gum disease, oral surgery, or children's practice.

Dentistry is a growing field in the United States and Canada. Dental hygienists have good opportunities in the field.

Managers run dental offices.

Words to Know

anatomy (uh-NAT-uh-mee)—the study of the body
decay (di-KAY)—a process that turns healthy teeth rotten
degree (di-GREE)—a title given to a person for completing a course of study
fluoride (FLOR-ide)—a chemical that helps prevent decay
infection (in-FEK-shuhn)—an illness caused by germs
license (LYE-suhnss)—a paper that gives permission to do something
specialize (SPESH-uh-lize)—to focus on one area of work
X ray (EKS-ray)—a photograph of the inside of a person's body

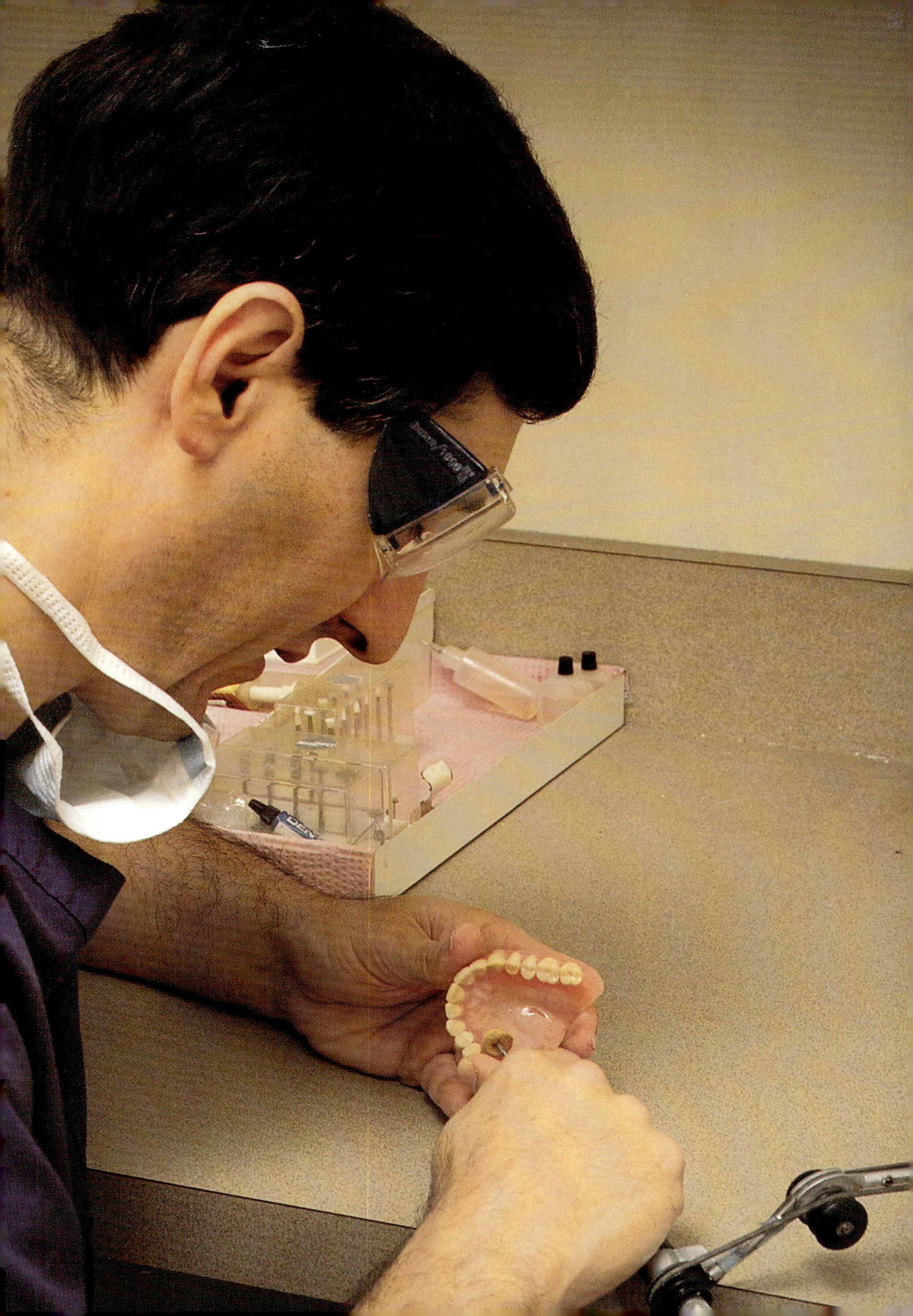

New Hampshire Board of Dental Examiners
This Certifies That
Rebecca A. Paskaley, R.D.H.
Dental Hygiene

To Learn More

Kendall, Bonnie. *Opportunities in Dental Care.* Lincolnwood, Ill.: VGM Career Books, 1991.

Rickert, Jessica A. *Careers in Dentistry.* New York: Rosen Group, 1996.

Smith, Ronald R. *Dental Hygienist.* (Smiths Career Notes Series). New York: R & E Publishers, 1993.

Wilkinson, Beth. *Careers Inside the World of Medicine.* New York: Rosen Group, 1995.

Useful Addresses

American Dental Association
211 E. Chicago Avenue
Chicago, IL 60611

American Dental Hygienists' Association
444 North Michigan Avenue
Suite 3400
Chicago, IL 60611

National Dental Hygienists' Association
5506 Connecticut Avenue
Suite 24-25
Washington, DC 20015

Internet Sites

American Association of Dental Schools (AADS)
http://www.aads.jhu.edu/

American Dental Association
http://www.ada.org/prac/careers/dc-menu.html

American Dental Hygienists' Association
http://www.adha.org

Dental Hygienists
http://stats.bl.gov/oco/ocos097.htm

Welcome to the Dental Site
http://www.dentalsite.com/

Index

anatomy, 23
associate's degree, 23

benefits, 31-33

calculus, 8
cavity, 8, 13
commission, 31-33

dentist, 7, 8, 10, 13, 16, 27, 34

floss, 8, 10
fluoride, 10

gum disease, 7, 10, 41

health insurance, 31

infection, 16

license, 24-27

outlook, 34

plaque, 8
preventive dentistry, 10

research, 18, 29, 31

salary, 31, 33, 38
sealant, 10

tooth decay, 7, 8, 10, 13

X ray, 13, 16

9708